7/28/23

D0208077

ECLIPSE OF
THE BODY

How We Lost the Meaning of Sex,
Gender, Marriage, & Family
(And How to Reclaim It)

CHRISTOPHER WEST

Totus Tuus
— P R E S S —
2018

Eclipse of the Body

Copyright © 2018 by Christopher West

Published by Totus Tuus Press
PO Box 5065
Scottsdale, AZ 85261

Cover design by Devin Schadt
Typesetting by Russell Design
Printed in the United States of America

ISBN: 978-1-944578-86-2
E book ISBN: 978-1-944578-87-9

INTRODUCTION

*If your whole body is full of light, and no part
of it is in darkness, then it will be as full of light as a
lamp illuminating you with its brightness.*
—Luke 11:36 (NABRE)

In our post-sexual revolution world, we are experiencing a total eclipse of the meaning of the body. Something is blocking the light and we simply no longer *see* the fundamental significance of the human body to human identity and human relationships.

Governments, in fact, are now demanding in law that we identify every-body without identifying anybody. But when we identify some-body without reference to his or her body, we identify, quite literally, no-body. In turn, a fork in the relationship between the human body and human identity creates a fork in the tongue.[1] Words like male and female, boy and girl, man and woman, sex and gender become meaningless. Separate the human body from human relationships and the meaning of words like husband and wife, father and mother, brother and sister, uncle and aunt also get totally eclipsed.

For most of human history, an eclipse of the sun was an ominous event. Before astronomers understood the phenomenon, inexplicable blackness in the middle of the day spelled the end of the world, until, of course, after a few minutes of sheer terror, the sun reappeared. What has passed in front of the light, blocking the body's meaning? Are there any "astronomers" out there who can explain this phenomenon, who can help us understand why this has happened and if, when, and how the darkness will pass? In this short book, I will point to three: Our Lady of Fatima, Pope Paul VI, and Pope St. John Paul II.

In Part I, I will demonstrate that "the beautiful woman from heaven" who appeared in Fatima, Portugal, in 1917 actually warned of the eclipse of the body that was coming upon the world. Then I will demonstrate how, building on the wisdom of the ages, Paul VI's encyclical *Of Human Life* (*Humanae Vitae*) properly recognized the modern embrace of contraception as the cause of the eclipse. In Part II, I will demonstrate how John Paul II's Theology of the Body provides a solid basis for hope that we won't remain in the darkness indefinitely; the eclipse of the body *will* pass when, as Mary promised, her Immaculate Heart triumphs.

PART I

THEY LOOK BUT DO NOT SEE

Our Lady of Fatima and the Errors of Russia

As most Catholics know, between May 13 and October 13, 1917, Mary appeared to three peasant children in Fatima, Portugal, and delivered a three-part message—the "three secrets" of Fatima, as they've come to be known. The first secret presented a horrifying vision of hell. The second involved a prophecy of World War II and the warning that "Russia would spread her errors throughout the world." However, Mary assured the children, "in the end" her Immaculate Heart would triumph and an "era of peace" would be granted to the world.

Mary also told the children that "the Holy Father will have much to suffer." This brings us to the third secret of Fatima, which was not publicly revealed until the year 2000, and which we will revisit later.

The errors of Russia mentioned in the second secret, rightly cause us to think of the spread of communism, the atheistic ideology based on Marxist economic theory.

As most of us learned in school, Karl Marx considered class struggle to be the defining factor of history. But digging deeper, Marx also believed that the fundamental "class struggle" was found in monogamous marriage and, indeed, in the sexual difference itself. "The first division of labor," Marx cowrote with Frederick Engels, "is that between man and woman for the propagation of children." In turn, Engels affirmed that Marxist theory "demands the abolition of the monogamous family as the economic unit of society."[2]

It seems the deeper revolution—and the deeper "error of Russia"—is the one aimed at destroying marriage and the family. In fact, much later in her life, Sister Lucia (the only of the three visionaries of Fatima to live beyond childhood; she died in 2005) wrote, "A time will come when the decisive battle between the kingdom of Christ and Satan will be over marriage and the family."[3] The modern agenda to deconstruct gender, marriage, and family life often draws straight from Marx. As feminist author Shulamith Firestone wrote in her 1970 manifesto *The Dialectic of Sex*: "And just as the end goal of socialist revolution was . . . the elimination of the . . . economic class *distinction* itself, so the end goal of feminist revolution must be . . . the elimination of . . . the sex *distinction* itself [so that] genital differences between human beings would no longer matter culturally." In this way, she asserted, "the tyranny of the biological family would be broken."

But what kind of revolution would be needed to render the sex distinction meaningless? To answer that question, we first need to understand the natural meaning and purpose of the sex distinction, more specifically, the meaning of genital difference.

The Facts of Life?

Imagine, if you will, that an alien being from a genderless galaxy landed on earth to study the human being. Coming from such a world, the male-female difference would likely be the *first* thing to catch its attention. "What is this difference *for*?" it would ask. Upon study, this alien would readily observe that each member of the human species is amazingly self-sufficient in his or her functions as an organism. The heart, the lungs, the kidney, the pancreas, the stomach, the bladder, the rectum, etc., all work together to carry out their functions. And both male and female have all the same organs . . . *except* . . . except what we fittingly call the *genital* organs.

There is one function this alien has discovered—and a critical function indeed—that simply cannot be carried out without cooperation from another member of the species. And that other member of the species *must* be of the opposite gender (that is, must have different, complementary genital organs), or said function doesn't function. This is the light that illuminates for the alien the most basic purpose of the gender difference. The genital organs of male and female actually *work together* in a stunning, harmonious interdependency to *generate* new members of the species. It's where we get the word *gender*, which, based on its Greek root, means "the manner in which one generates." We see the same root in words like *genesis*, *generous*, *genitals*, *progeny*, *genes*, and *genealogy*.

Furthermore, since the child born to them cannot survive on its own, the alien rightly realizes that the man and the woman who cooperated in generating this new life, if they are to be responsible, must commit themselves to rearing their child. Precisely *this* commitment—the commitment to responsible genital intercourse as the foundation of future generations—is called marriage.

It used to be obvious to everyone: genitals are meant to generate. We called it "the facts of life." But today those facts are entirely up for grabs, and the fundamental link between gender, genitals, and generating has all but vanished from the way we understand ourselves and our genital relationships. As a culture, we are desperately in need of recovering what should be an obvious and celebrated truth: *sex leads to babies.* Tragically, as I will demonstrate, when we fail to respect the fact that genitals are meant to generate, we begin to degenerate.

The Crack in the Dam

How did we as a culture come to forget—or, rather, dismiss—the fact that genitals are meant to generate? Since the beginning of history men and women have sought ways—usually crude and ineffective ways—of thwarting the generative power of their genitals. However, only with the vulcanization of rubber in the mid-1800s, and then with the invention of the Pill a century later, did we have consistently reliable ways of doing so.

Still, if a true contraceptive revolution was to occur, it needed not only new technologies, but new mentalities. As difficult as it may be for us to imagine today, contraception in much of the Western world was not only frowned upon at the turn of the twentieth century as immoral; it was also illegal. Those who campaigned for its acceptance knew they would make little progress without the "blessing" of Christian leaders. Few today realize that, until 1930, all Christian denominations were unanimous in their firm opposition to any attempt to separate genitals from generating. That year, the Anglican Church succumbed to pressure and opened the door to contraception at its Lambeth Conference. In doing so, it became the first Christian body to break with the continuous teaching of the early Church, the saints throughout the ages, and all the Reformers from Luther to Calvin and beyond.

Within a matter of weeks, Pope Pius XI responded as follows:

> Since, therefore, openly departing from the uninterrupted Christian tradition some recently have judged it possible solemnly to declare another doctrine regarding this question, the Catholic Church . . . raises her voice in token of her divine ambassadorship and . . . proclaims anew: any use whatsoever of matrimony exercised in such a way that the act is deliberately frustrated in its natural power to generate life is an offence against the law of God and of nature.[4]

In the years that followed, every major Protestant denomination shifted from condemning contraception to not only accepting it, but advocating it. Unimaginable global pressure was now being put on the Catholic Church to follow suit, and it seemed to many that it was having its desired effect. In the early 1960s, the Fathers of the Second Vatican Council stated that they reserved judgment on certain "questions which need further and more careful investigation." These "have been handed over . . . to a commission for the study of population, family, and births, in order that, after it fulfills its function, the Supreme Pontiff may pass judgment."[5]

The point in question was the birth control pill, a new technology at the time that seemed to some not to qualify under the traditional teaching against contraception. The council's tacit admission of uncertainty on this point gave people the impression that a papal blessing on the Pill was forthcoming. In fact, the majority of the papal commission studying the question advised Pope Paul VI not only to accept the Pill, but to follow the lead of other Christian communities and change Church teaching on contraception all together. When the Majority Report was leaked to the press in early May 1967, there was a sense of certainty that a change in teaching was immanent. One week later, Paul VI visited Fatima. He came on Our Lady of Fatima's feast day (May 13) and prayed specifically against "new ideologies" that were threatening the Church by introducing a "profane mentality" and "worldly morals."[6]

A little over a year later, on July 25, 1968, Paul VI shocked the world when he issued his encyclical letter *Of Human Life* (*Humanae Vitae*), reaffirming the traditional Christian teaching against contraception, including the Pill. Although he was mocked and scorned globally—both from outside and, sadly, from within the Church—his words were prescient. He warned that a contracepting world becomes a world of rampant infidelity; a world where women and childbearing are degraded; a world in which governments trample on the rights and needs of the family; and a world in which human beings believe they can manipulate their bodies at will.[7] In other words, Paul VI showed himself to be an "astronomer" who understood the power of contraception to eclipse the meaning of the body, casting a dark shadow over the meaning of the gender difference itself, and hence, the meaning of marriage and the family.

Wise men and women throughout history have always understood that fertility was the light that illuminated the sexual relationship, and that rendering it sterile would cast a long shadow over civilization. In fact, when Margaret Sanger first started her global campaigns for contraception in the early 1900s, there was no shortage of predictions that embracing contraception would lead to the societal chaos in which we're now immersed. You might be just as surprised as I was to read what the following prominent thinkers of the early twentieth century had to say about contraception and what they predicted would happen if we embraced it.

Sigmund Freud, for example, while he was clearly no friend of religion, understood that the "abandonment of the reproductive function is the common feature of all perversions. We actually describe a sexual activity as perverse," he said, "if it has given up the aim of reproduction and pursues the attainment of pleasure as an aim independent of it."[8]

Theodore Roosevelt condemned contraception as a serious threat against the welfare of the nation, describing it as "the one sin for which the penalty is national death, race death; a sin for which there is no atonement."[9]

Gandhi insisted that contraceptive methods are "like putting a premium on vice. They make man and woman reckless." He predicted that nature "will have full revenge for any such violation of her laws. Moral results can only be produced by moral restraints." Hence, if contraceptive methods "become the order of the day, nothing but moral degradation can be the result. . . . As it is, man has sufficiently degraded woman for his lust, and [contraception], no matter how well meaning the advocates may be, will still further degrade her."[10]

When a committee of the Federal Council of Churches in America issued a report suggesting it follow the Anglican acceptance of contraception, *The Washington Post* published a stinging editorial with the following prophetic statement: "Carried to its logical conclusions, the committee's report if carried into effect would sound the death knell of marriage as a holy institution by establishing degrading practices which would encourage indiscriminate immorality. The suggestion that the use of legalized contraceptives would be 'careful and restrained' is preposterous."[11]

Also in response to the Anglican break with Christian moral teaching, T.S. Eliot insisted that the church "is trying the experiment of attempting to form a civilized but non-Christian mentality. The experiment will fail; but we must be very patient in waiting the collapse; meanwhile redeeming the time: so that the Faith may be preserved alive through the dark ages before us; to renew and rebuild civilization and save the World from suicide."[12]

Perversity? National death? Moral degradation? The death of marriage as a holy institution? World suicide? Isn't that a bit much to pin on contraception? It would certainly seem so, if it weren't for the fact that much of what these forecasters predicted has, indeed, come to pass. What did they understand that we have forgotten?

Untying the Tight-Knot Nexus

Civil law used to understand, defend, and protect the fact that marriage, sex, and babies belong together . . . and in that order. In the age-old Christian understanding, God, in his loving design, has united these three realities in a tight knot to reveal in our flesh the truth of his own eternal covenant love and Fatherhood. Contraception not only loosens the knot of this fundamental and society-ordering nexus, it cuts the ties.

Separate sex from babies and you also separate sex from marriage—both in principle and in practice. So long as the natural connection between sex and babies is retained, we realize intuitively that sexual intercourse is the domain of those who have committed themselves to raising children: that commitment, as our alien friend realized earlier, is called marriage. Insert contraception into the tight-knot nexus of marriage-sex-babies and everything will start to unravel as follows.

The temptation to commit adultery is certainly nothing new. However, one of the main deterrents throughout history to succumbing to the temptation has been the fear of an unwanted pregnancy. That's the tight-knot nexus of marriage-sex-babies doing its job. What would happen to rates of adultery in a given population if we untied that knot with contraception? Incidents of infidelity would be sure to rise. What happens when incidents of infidelity rise? Rates of marital breakdown and divorce rise.

It gets worse. The temptation to engage in sex before marriage is nothing new. However, as with adultery, one of the main deterrents throughout history to succumbing to the temptation has been the fear of unwanted pregnancy. Once again, that's the tight-knot nexus doing its job. What would happen to rates of premarital sex in a given population if we untied that knot with contraception? They would certainly rise.

It gets worse. Since no method of contraception is 100 percent effective, an increase in adultery and premarital sex in a given population will inevitably lead to an increase in unwanted pregnancies. What happens when large numbers of women find themselves pregnant and didn't want to be? Demand for a legal "right" to abortion logically follows as a way of solving this problem.

The common wisdom is that better access to contraception decreases rates of abortion. But even a cursory look at the data shows that in every nation that has embraced contraception, abortions have multiplied, not diminished. Once we've severed the knot uniting marriage, sex, and babies, we don't like it when nature's nexus reasserts itself. The initial impulse to indulge libido without commitment and without consequence now morphs into a *demand* to be "free" to do so, even at the cost of extinguishing an innocent human life. While there's an initial logic to the idea that contraception curbs abortion, when we take a deeper look we realize that trying to solve the latter (abortion) with the former (contraception) is like throwing gasoline on a fire to try to put it out. In the final analysis, there is only one reason we have abortion: because people have rejected the God-given purpose of sex; because they've sought to separate genitals from generating. Contraception doesn't solve that problem; it fosters it.

It gets worse. Not everyone will resort to abortion, of course—thanks be to God for that. Some will offer their children up for adoption, a heroic decision. Most mothers, however, will raise these children on their own. This, too, can be heroic, but now the number of children who grow up without a father—which has already been increased by the rise in divorce (brought on by the rise in adultery, brought on by the acceptance of contraception)—will be compounded.

Certainly God's grace can supply what is lacking and those raised without a father can lead healthy, holy lives. Still, as numerous studies (and common sense) indicate, the chances are dramatically higher that "fatherless" children will: grow up in poverty; have emotional, psychological, and behavioral problems; suffer poor health; drop out of school; engage in premarital sex; obtain abortions; do drugs; commit violent crimes; and end up in jail. All of these social ills compound exponentially from generation to generation, since "fatherless" children are also much more likely to have out-of-wedlock births and, if they marry at all, to divorce.

Redefining Marriage, Sex, and Babies

As history clearly shows, when we begin untying the tight-knot nexus of marriage, sex, and babies, we end up redefining all three. Babies become mere "clumps of cells." Sex becomes mere uncommitted pleasure exchange between consenting partners (gender being irrelevant and malleable). And marriage becomes a demanded societal and governmental "stamp of approval" on one's preferred relationship and method of sexual pleasure exchange.

And this is why embracing contraception has led, as a matter of course, to the normalization of homosexual behavior: once you sever orgasm from procreation, why does orgasm need to be an experience limited to the opposite sex? Deliberately sterilizing sexual intercourse effectively nullifies the natural and essential meaning of the sexual difference. When we recognize this, we come to see the hard truth that Christians themselves unwittingly began to "homo-sexualize" marriage when they began to embrace contraception.

In truth, it's impossible to *raise* what two men or two women might do with their genitals to the level of what God invites a man and a woman to do with their genitals in marriage: generate the next generation. But it *is* possible to *reduce* what men and women do with their genitals in marriage to what same-sex couples do with theirs: engage in the pursuit of sterile pleasure. That's what contraception has done to marriage: it has *reduced* it to the same thing pursued in same-sex unions. Hence, when married couples claim a "right" to sterilize their union, it is only a matter of time before those inclined to inherently sterile unions (i.e., same-sex unions) claim a "right" to marry on the basis of "equality." When the essential meaning of the genital difference is eclipsed by a contraceptive mentality, the genital activities of opposite-sex couples and same-sex couples do, indeed, become "the same thing," as those who have successfully campaigned for "marriage equality" have insisted.

Seventy-two years after the 1930 Anglican decision, Archbishop of Canterbury Rowan Williams observed that "the absolute condemnation of same-sex relations" has nothing substantial to rely upon in "a church that accepts the legitimacy of contraception."[13] He was correct. But rather than question the legitimacy of contraception, he took that as a given and justified homosexual behavior. If we are being logically consistent, it has to be one or the other.

In a 1984 interview, the future pope Benedict XVI predicted that we will atone in our day for "the consequences of a sexuality which is no longer linked to . . . procreation. It logically follows from this that every form of [genital activity] is equivalent. . . . No longer having an objective reason to justify it, sex seeks the subjective reason in the gratification of the desire, in the most 'satisfying' answer for the individual." In turn, he observed that everyone becomes "free to give to his personal *libido* the content considered suitable for himself. . . . Hence, it naturally follows that all forms of sexual gratification are transformed into the 'rights' of the individual." From there, he concluded that people end up demanding the right of "escaping from the 'slavery of nature,' demanding the right to be male or female at one's will or pleasure."[14]

Who can deny that this is the world we live in today?

PART II

COME, AND BECOME ONE WHO SEES

We Need a "Total Vision of Man"

Soon after Pope Paul VI died in August 1978, the cardinal archbishop of Krakow came to Rome to help elect a new pope. He brought with him a lengthy handwritten manuscript that he had been prayerfully crafting for nearly four years. It was almost complete and he wished to work on it, when he could, during the conclave. Page 1 bore the unusual title (in Polish): "*teologia ciala*"—"theology of the body." The hundreds of pages that followed held perhaps the most profound and compelling biblical reflection on the meaning of our creation and redemption as male and female ever articulated—the in-depth mystical insights of a modern saint that had the power to change the world, *if* those insights had an opportunity to reach the world, that is.

After the election of Pope John Paul I, Cardinal Wojtyla returned to Krakow and completed his manuscript. Soon after that, to the astonishment of the whole world, he emerged from the second conclave of 1978 as Pope John Paul II. And his "theology of the body"—delivered as a series of 129[15] Wednesday talks between September 1979 and November 1984 rather than being published as a book—became the first major teaching project of his pontificate.

John Paul II's Theology of the Body (hereafter, TOB) was inspired by something Paul VI had said in *Humanae Vitae*: he had observed that, in order to understand Christian teaching on sex and procreation, we must look "beyond partial perspectives" to an "integral vision of man and of his vocation."[16] This is what John Paul II set out to do in his TOB—provide the integral or total vision of man that would enable us to understand and live joyfully the Church's teaching on the meaning and purpose *of human life (humanae vitae)*.

The operative term here is *vision*. John Paul II understood that, while the people of the modern world were obsessed with looking at the human body, "They look but do not see" (Matt 13:13 NABRE). His TOB was an invitation to every human being to "Come, and become one who sees" (cf. John 1:39).[17]

Inadequate legalistic formulations of moral theology coupled with disparaging treatments of sexual matters by some previous churchmen had led countless people to turn a deaf ear to the Church whenever she spoke on sexual matters. John Paul II was confident, however, that he had something to say that could make a difference. He believed he could demonstrate that *Humanae Vitae* was not against man but unstintingly *for* him; that *Humanae Vitae* was not opposed to erotic love and sexual pleasure, but called men and women to the most spiritually intense experiences of them. To get there, however, questions surrounding sexual morality needed to be reframed. Instead of asking, "How far can I go before I break the law?" we need to ask, "What does it mean to be human?" "What is a person?" "What does it mean to love?" "Why did God make me male or female?" "Why did God create sex in the first place?"

In short, John Paul II's long-studied answer to that final question is this: human sexuality is a sign—in fact, a sacramental sign—that's meant to proclaim, reveal, and enable human beings to participate in the "great mystery" hidden in God from all eternity.

The Sacramentality of the Body

How can we describe the "great mystery" of the sacraments? They are the physical means through which we encounter God's spiritual treasures. In the sacraments, spirit and matter "kiss." Heaven and earth embrace in a marriage that will never end. The human body itself is in some sense a "sacrament." Rather than referring to the seven signs of grace that Christ instituted, when John Paul II speaks of the body as a sacrament, he means it is a sign that somehow makes visible the invisible mystery of God.

We cannot see God. God is pure spirit. And yet, St. John the Evangelist tells us that God's life was made visible. Speaking of "the word of life," the mystery which "was from the beginning," John claimed that he and his companions had *seen* this mystery "with our eyes" and had touched it "with our hands" (1 John 1:1–2). Christianity is the religion of God's self-disclosure. God wants to reveal himself to us. He wants to make his invisible, spiritual mystery visible to us so that we can "see" him and "touch" him. How does he do so?

God speaks to us in sign language, revealing himself through the veil of this physical world. Most everyone has experienced that deep sense of awe and wonder in beholding a starlit night or a radiant sunset or a beautiful flower. In these moments, whether we realize it or not, we are reading God's sign language, seeing God's goodness and beauty reflected in his creation. "The beauty of creation reflects the infinite beauty of the Creator," as the *Catechism of the Catholic Church* puts it (CCC 341).

And yet there's something more grand than any starlit night, sunset, or flower. There's something at the pinnacle of creation that God designed in order to speak his sign language more potently, more poignantly than anything else: "God created man in his own image, in the image of God he created him; male and female he created them. And God blessed them and said to them, 'Be fruitful and multiply'" (Gen 1:27–28). To say "theology of the body," is, in fact, just another way of saying we're made in the image and likeness of God.

Precisely in our creation as male and female and in our call to fruitful communion, the human body becomes the greatest sign of the spiritual and the divine. And the more we learn how to read this sign, the more we enter into the "great mystery" of who God is and what his eternal plan is for the human race.

John Paul II's Thesis

This brings us to the thesis statement of John Paul II's TOB, the brush with which he paints his entire vision:

> The body, in fact, and only the body, is capable of making visible what is invisible: the spiritual and divine. It has been created to transfer into the visible reality of the world the mystery hidden from eternity in God, and thus to be a sign of it (TOB 19:4).

Let's begin unpacking this dense statement. Think of your own experiences as a human being: Your body is not just a shell in which you dwell. Your body is not just *a* body. Your body is not just *any* body. Your body is *some*body—you! Through the profound unity of your body and your soul, your body *reveals* or makes visible the invisible reality of your spiritual soul. The "you" you are is not just a soul "in" a body. Your body is not something you have or own alongside yourself. Your body *is* you. This is why if someone broke your jaw in a fit of rage, you wouldn't take him to court for property damage, but for personal assault. What we do to our bodies, we do to ourselves; and what is done to our bodies is done to ourselves.

Once again, our bodies make visible what is invisible—the spiritual *and the divine*. It's from this perspective that John Paul II studies the human body—not merely as a biological organism, but as a *theology*, as a "study of God."

The body is not divine, of course. But it *is* the most powerful sign of the divine mystery in all creation. A sign is something that points us to a reality beyond itself and, in some way, makes that transcendent reality present to us. The divine mystery always remains infinitely "beyond"; it cannot be reduced to its sign. Yet the sign is indispensable in making visible the invisible mystery. As the *Catechism* says, "Man needs signs and symbols to communicate. . . . The same holds true for his relationship with God" (CCC 1146).

Tragically, because of sin, the "body loses its character as a sign" (TOB 40:4)—not objectively, but subjectively. In other words, in itself the body retains its character as a sign of the spiritual and divine, but we've been blinded to it. We "look but do not see" (Matt 13:13 NABRE). As a result, we tend to consider the human body merely as a physical "thing" entirely separated from the spiritual and the divine. And this is why the very expression "theology of the body" seems so odd to people today, even to Christians. It shouldn't, if we believe in the Incarnation. As John Paul II put it: "Through the fact that the Word of God became flesh, the body entered theology . . . through the main door" (TOB 23:4).

Everything in Christianity hinges on the Incarnation. God's mystery has been revealed in human flesh, rendering the human body a study of God, a *theology*. "Theology of the body," therefore, is not merely the title of a series of papal talks on sex and marriage; theology of the body is the very logic of Christianity. For in "the body of Jesus 'we see our God made visible and so are caught up in love of the God we cannot see'" (CCC 477).

The Divine Mystery

Several times already we have spoken of the divine mystery or the mystery hidden in God from all eternity (see Eph 3:9). What does this mean? In the Christian sense, "mystery" does not refer to an unsolvable puzzle. It refers to the innermost "secret" of God and to his eternal plan for humanity. These realities are so far beyond anything we can comprehend that all we can really utter is the word "mystery." And yet God's secret is knowable—not based on our ability to decipher a divine puzzle, but because God has made it known.

As the *Catechism* says, "God has revealed his innermost secret: God himself is an eternal exchange of love, Father, Son, and Holy Spirit, and he has destined us to share in that exchange" (CCC 221). God is not a tyrant; God is not a slave driver; God is not merely a legislator or lawgiver; and he's certainly not an old man with a white beard waiting to strike us down whenever we fail. God is an "eternal exchange of love." He's an infinite Communion of Persons experiencing eternal love-bliss. And he created us for one reason: to share that eternal love and bliss with us.

This is what makes the Gospel *Good News*: there is a banquet of love that corresponds to the hungry cry of our hearts, and it is God's free gift to us! We needn't climb some high mountain to find it. We needn't cross the sea. The "great mystery" of God's love is very close to us, intimately part of us. Indeed, God inscribed an image of this "great mystery" in the very form of our bodies by making us male and female and calling the two to become one flesh.

The Spousal Analogy

Scripture uses many images to help us understand God's love. Each has its own valuable place. But, as

John Paul II wrote, the gift of Christ's body on the cross gives "definitive prominence to the spousal meaning of God's love."[18] In fact, from beginning to end, in the mysteries of our creation, fall, and redemption, the Bible tells a nuptial or marital story.

It begins in Genesis with the marriage of the first man and woman, and it ends in Revelation with the marriage of Christ and the Church. Right in the middle of the Bible we find the erotic poetry of the Song of Songs. These bookends and this centerpiece provide the key for reading the whole biblical story. Indeed, we can summarize all of Sacred Scripture with five simple yet astounding words: *God wants to marry us.*

> For as a young man marries a virgin, your Builder shall marry you; And as a bridegroom rejoices in his bride so shall your God rejoice in you (Isa 62:5 NABRE).

God is inviting each of us, in a unique and unrepeatable way, to an unimagined intimacy with him, akin to the intimacy of spouses in one flesh. While we may need to work through some discomfort or fear here to reclaim the true sacredness, the true holiness of the imagery, the "scandalous" truth is that Scripture describes "God's passion for his people using boldly erotic images," as Pope Benedict XVI put it.[19] Elsewhere he declared: "Eros is part of God's very Heart: the Almighty awaits the 'yes' of his creatures as a young bridegroom that of his bride."[20]

We are probably more familiar (and more comfortable) describing God's love as *agape*—the Greek word that typically describes sacrificial, self-giving love. Yet God's love "may certainly be called *eros*," asserts Benedict XVI. In Christ *eros* is "supremely ennobled . . . so purified as to become one with *agape*." Thus, the Bible has no qualms employing the erotic poetry of the Song of Songs as a description of "God's relation to man and man's relation to God." In this way, as Benedict XVI concludes, the Song of Songs became not only an expression of the intimacies of marital love, it also became "an expression of the essence of biblical faith: that man can indeed enter into union with God—his primordial aspiration."[21]

The Essence of Biblical Faith

The above statement demands careful and prayerful reflection: this unabashed celebration of erotic love (the Song of Songs) expresses the essence of biblical faith? How so? The essence of biblical faith is that God came among us in the flesh not only to forgive our sins (as astounding as that gift is); he became "one flesh" with us so that we could share in his eternal exchange of love. In the first of his many sermons on the Song of

Songs, St. Bernard of Clairvaux aptly describes marriage as "the sacrament of endless union with God." Revelation calls this endless union the "marriage of the Lamb" (Rev 19:7).

But there's more. Not only does God love us; not only does he want to marry us. . . . Remember that pithy rhyme we learned as children: "First comes love, then comes marriage, then comes the baby in the baby carriage"? We probably didn't realize that we were actually reciting some profound *theology*: theology *of the body!* Our bodies tell the story that God loves us, wants to marry us, and wants us to "conceive" eternal life within us. "What is happening here?" asks St. Bonaventure. When God fills us with his divine life, it is "nothing other than the heavenly Father by a divine seed, as it were, impregnating the soul and making it fruitful."[22]

For Christians, the idea of divine impregnation is not merely a metaphor. Representing all of us, a young Jewish woman named Mary once gave her "yes" to God's marriage proposal with such totality and fidelity that she literally conceived eternal life in her womb. In a hymn addressed to her, St. Augustine exclaims: "The Word becomes united with flesh, he makes his covenant with flesh, and your womb is the sacred bed on which this holy union of the Word with flesh is consummated."[23] Mary's virginity has always been understood by the Church as the sign of her betrothal to God. She is the "mystic bride of love eternal," as a traditional hymn has it. As such, Mary perfectly fulfills the spousal character of the human vocation in relation to God (see CCC 505).

In turn, Mary fully illuminates the theology of a woman's body. In her, woman's body has literally become the dwelling place of the Most High God—heaven on earth! Every woman shares in some way in this incomparable dignity and calling. Every woman's body is a sign of heaven on earth. And, oh, how lovely is your dwelling place, Lord, mighty God (see Ps 84:1). Continue unfolding this astounding mystery and it is not difficult to recognize that the theology of a man's body can be described as a call to enter the gates of heaven, to surrender himself there, to lay down his life there by pouring himself out utterly. In this way the man images the eternal outpouring, the eternal life-givingness of God as Father.

Can we even imagine a greater sacredness, a greater holiness, a greater goodness and glory ascribed to our maleness and femaleness, our sexuality? Oh, Lord, show us who we really are! Give us eyes to see so glorious a mystery revealed through our bodies and in the call of man and woman to become one flesh!

Penetrating the Essence of the Mystery
In the midst of unfolding the biblical analogy of spousal love, it's very important to understand the bounds

within which we're using such language and imagery. "It is obvious," writes John Paul II, "that the analogy of . . . human spousal love, cannot offer an adequate and complete understanding of . . . the divine mystery." God's "*mystery* remains *transcendent with respect to this analogy* as with respect to any other analogy." At the same time, however, John Paul II maintains that the spousal analogy allows a certain "penetration" into the very essence of the mystery (see TOB 95b:1). And no biblical author reaches more deeply into this essence than St. Paul in his letter to the Ephesians.

Quoting directly from Genesis, Paul states: "'For this reason a man shall leave his father and mother and be joined to his wife, and the two shall become one flesh.'" Then, linking the original marriage with the ultimate marriage, he adds: "This is a great mystery, and I mean in reference to Christ and the church" (Eph 5:31–32).

We can hardly overstate the importance of this passage for John Paul II and the whole theological tradition of the Church. He calls it the "summa" of Christian teaching about who God is and who we are.[24] He says this passage contains the "crowning" of all the themes in Sacred Scripture and expresses the "central reality" of the whole of divine revelation (see TOB 87:3). The mystery spoken of in this passage "is *'great' indeed*," he says. "It is what God . . . wishes above all to transmit to mankind in his Word." Thus, "one can say that [this] passage

. . . 'reveals—in a particular way—*man to man himself* and makes *his supreme vocation* clear'" (TOB 93:2; 87:6).

So what is this "supreme vocation" we have as human beings that Ephesians 5 makes clear? Stammering for words to describe the ineffable, the mystics call it "nuptial union" . . . *with the Infinite.*[25] Christ is the new Adam who left his Father in heaven. He also left the home of his mother on earth. Why? To mount "the marriage bed of the cross," as St. Augustine had it, unite himself with the Church, symbolized by "the woman" at the foot of the cross, and consummate the union forever. Archbishop Fulton Sheen elaborates:

> Now we've always thought, and rightly so, of Christ the Son on the cross and the mother beneath him. But that's not the complete picture. That's not the deep understanding. Who is our Lord on the cross? He's the new Adam. Where's the new Eve? At the foot of the cross . . . If Eve became the mother of the living in the natural order, is not this woman at the foot of the cross to become another mother? [How does this spiritual motherhood happen?] . . . As St. Augustine puts it, and here I am quoting him verbatim, ". . . As it were, the blood and water that came from the side of Christ was the spiritual seminal fluid." And so from these nuptials "Woman, there's your son" this is the beginning of the Church.[26]

"On the Cross, God's eros for us is made manifest," proclaims Benedict XVI. "Eros is indeed . . . that force which 'does not allow the lover to remain in himself but moves him to become one with the beloved.' Is there more 'mad eros' . . . than that which led the Son of God to make himself one with us even to the point of suffering as his own the consequences of our offenses?" he asks.[27]

The more we allow the brilliant rays of Christ's "mad eros" to illuminate our vision, the more we come to understand, as the *Catechism* observes, how the "entire Christian life bears the mark of the spousal love of Christ and the Church. Already Baptism, the entry into the People of God, is a nuptial mystery" (CCC 1617). Here "the 'imperishable seed' of the Word of God produces its life-giving effect" (CCC 1228). The "imperishable seed" is given by Christ as Bridegroom and received by the Church as Bride. And through these glorious, virginal nuptials the Church brings forth sons and daughters "to a new and immortal life" (CCC 507).

Still, as glorious as baptism is, it's only our entry into the Christian life, not its summit. Baptism opens the way to the sacrament of sacraments, the mystery of mysteries; baptism "is so to speak the nuptial bath which precedes the wedding feast, the Eucharist" (CCC 1617).

The Summit of the Spousal Analogy

In the Eucharist, "Christ is united with his 'body' as

the bridegroom with the bride," John Paul II tells us. As such, the Eucharist illuminates with supernatural brilliance "the relationship between man and woman, between what is 'feminine' and what is 'masculine.'"[28] It is in the Eucharist that the meaning of life, love, sex, gender, and marriage is fully revealed! How so?

There is such a strong temptation to disincarnate and, thus, neuter our faith that we're often oblivious to the profound significance of the fact that there is a *man* on the cross and a *woman* at the foot of the cross. It can't be the other way around. In the spousal analogy, God is always the Bridegroom and humanity is always the Bride. Why? Because humanity is first receptive to the love of God: "In this is love, not that we loved God but that he loved us" (1 John 4:10). The woman's body primarily tells the story of *receiving* divine love while the man's body primarily tells the story of *offering* that love, of pouring it out.

The more we press in to this divine love story, the more we realize why only a man can be an ordained priest: It's the bridegroom who gives the seed or inseminates; it's the bride who receives the seed within and conceives new life. This is why a man trains to be a priest in the *seminary* and, once ordained, is called *Father*. A woman cannot be ordained a priest because she is not ordained by God to be a father; she is ordained by God to be a mother. This is where the sexual difference matters—in the call to holy communion and generation. If a woman were to attempt to confer the Eucharist, the relationship would be bride to bride. There would be no possibility of Holy Communion and no possibility of generating new life.

Of course, a world that insists two women can marry will also insist that a woman can be ordained a priest, but both ideas come from the same failure to recognize the essential meaning of the gender distinction. Recall that gender means the manner in which one generates, which is based on one's genitals. When men generate (in the manner in which only men generate), they become fathers. When women generate (in the manner in which only women generate), they become mothers. And both *need* the other in order to generate at all. This is all readily apparent . . . *unless* . . . unless we have eclipsed the meaning of gender with a contraceptive mentality. Rob the genitals of their ability to generate and the natural purpose of the gender distinction is lost. In turn, since grace builds on nature, when we're confused about the natural reality, we're also confused about the supernatural reality: "If I have told you earthly things and you do not believe," asks Jesus, "how can you believe if I tell you heavenly things?" (John 3:12).

The more deeply we enter into the "great mystery" of Ephesians 5, the more we will see how and why the gender difference is just as important to the Holy Communion of the Eucharist as it is to the holy communion of marriage. In fact, as John Paul II teaches, we cannot understand one without the other. Perhaps the following story will illuminate what he means. I never met my father-in-law, he died when my wife was a girl, but I admire him tremendously because of the intuition he had as a brand new husband. At Mass the day after his wedding, having consummated his marriage the night before, he was in tears as he came back to the pew after receiving the Eucharist. When his new bride inquired, he said, "For the first time in my life I understood the meaning of those words, 'This is my body given for you.'"

Make no mistake: when all the confusion is cast out and all the distortions are untwisted, the deepest meaning and purpose of human sexuality is to point us to the Eucharist, the "marriage supper of the Lamb" (Rev 19:9). And this is precisely why questions of sex, gender, and marriage place us right in the center of "the situation in which *the powers of good and evil fight against each other*" (TOB 115:2).

The Body and the Spiritual Battle

If God created the body and sexual union to proclaim his own eternal mystery of love, why do we not typically see and experience them in this profound way? For example, when you hear the word "sex," what generally comes to mind? Is it the great mystery of Ephesians 5 . . . or is it something, shall we say, a little less sacred than that? Remember, it's because of sin that the "body loses its character as a sign" of the divine mystery (see TOB 40:4).

Ponder this for a moment: if the union of the sexes is the original sign in this world of our call to union with God, and if there is an enemy who wants to separate us from God, where do you think he's going to aim his most potent arrows? If we want to know what is most sacred in this world, all we need do is look for what is most violently profaned.

It is sobering in the utmost to think that all the sexual chaos and gender confusion in our world today might be the unfolding of a diabolic plot to keep us from union with God. This much is certain from Paul's letter to the Ephesians: The battle for man's soul is fought over the truth of his body. It's no mere coincidence that Paul follows his presentation of the ultimate meaning of gender, sex, and marriage in Ephesians 5 with his call to spiritual warfare in Ephesians 6. These issues place us "at the center of the great struggle between good and evil, between life and death, between love and all that is opposed to love."[29] That's why the first thing we must do to win this battle is gird [our] loins with the truth (see Eph 6:14).

The TOB is John Paul II's clarion call for all men and women to do just that—to gird their loins with the truth that will set them free to love; the truth that will reunite men and women with one another in the image of God and, thus, reunite them with God himself. We must ask ourselves: are our loins girded in the truth, or are they girded in latex?

Ethics of the Sign

We can argue against contraception with philosophical reasoning alone, without any appeal to faith or the Bible. But John Paul II's project was to show the deepest *theological* reason for the immorality of contraception. Here it is: rendering the one-flesh union sterile falsifies the sacramental sign of married love. It violates what John Paul II calls "the ethics of the sign."

As a sacrament, marriage not only signifies God's life and love, it *really participates* in God's life and love—or, at least, it's meant to do so. For sacraments to convey grace (God's life and love), the sacramental sign must accurately signify the spiritual mystery. For example, as a physical sign of cleansing, the waters of baptism really and truly bring about a spiritual cleansing from sin. But if you were to baptize someone with mud or tar, no spiritual cleansing would take place because the physical sign is now one of making dirty. This would actually be a countersign of the spiritual reality of baptism.

All of married life is a sacrament. All of married life is meant to be a sign of God's life and love. But this sacrament has a consummate expression. Sexual intercourse is the full-bodied sign language of God's love. Here, like no other moment in married life, spouses are invited to participate in the "great mystery" of God's creative and redemptive love. But this will only happen if their sexual union accurately *signifies* God's love. Therefore, as John Paul II concludes, we can speak of moral good and evil in the sexual relationship based on whether the couple gives to their union "the character of a truthful sign" (TOB 37:6).

As John Paul II's TOB so brilliantly illuminates, the human body has a language written by God into the mystery of the sexual difference: it is meant to proclaim the truth of divine love and enable men and women to participate in it. But as with any language, it is possible to speak the truth with the body and it is also possible to speak lies.

The essential element for marriage to be a "true sign"—an authentic sacrament—is the language of the body spoken in truth. This is precisely how spouses "constitute" the sacramental sign of marriage (see TOB 104:9). By participating in God's eternal plan of love, John Paul II even insists that the language of the body becomes "prophetic." However, we must be careful to distinguish true and false prophets. As John Paul II observes, the teaching of *Humanae Vitae* simply carries this truth to its logical conclusions (see TOB 123:2).

Insert contraception into the language of the body and (knowingly or unknowingly) the couple engages in a countersign of the "great mystery." Rather than proclaiming "God is life-giving love," the language of contracepted intercourse says, "God is *not* life-giving love." In this way spouses (knowingly or unknowingly) become "false prophets." They blaspheme. Their bodies are still proclaiming a theology, but it's a theology that falsifies divine love.

Incarnating Divine Love

"Love one another as I have loved you" (John 15:12). This "new commandment" of Jesus summarizes the very meaning of life. It's a commandment that God inscribed right from the beginning not in stone tablets, but in the very mystery of our bodies, in the very mysteries of sex, gender, and marriage.

How did Christ love us? "This is my body . . . given for you . . . This cup is the new covenant in my blood, which is poured out for you" (Luke 22:19–20 NABRE). These are the Lord's wedding vows, offered to his Bride at the Last Supper as a verbal expression of the language of his heart. Then, when he lay down on "the marriage bed of the cross," he expressed the same covenant love without words, through the language of his body. In this way, Christ the Bridegroom showed us "to the end" what spousal love *is*, what it calls us to, what it demands of us, and, through his Resurrection, what it rewards those who—notwithstanding their own limitations, weaknesses, and sins—entrust themselves to God's grace and mercy and embrace the truth of spousal love with all their hearts.

Without that entrustment to God's grace and mercy, those same limitations, weaknesses, and sins incline us very powerfully toward a "love" that is riddled with selfishness and egoism. Thus, we must constantly challenge ourselves to distinguish true love from its many distortions and falsifications by measuring everything we call "love" against Christ's love.

How does Christ love? First, he gives himself *freely* ("No one takes [my life] from me, but I lay it down of my own accord"—John 10:18). Second, he gives himself *totally*: without reservation, condition, or selfish calculation ("He loved them to the end"—John 13:1). Third, he gives himself *faithfully* ("I am with you always"— Matt 28:20). And fourth, he gives himself *fruitfully* ("I came that they may have life"—John 10:10). If men and women are to speak the true language of their bodies, they must learn continually and ever more deeply to open themselves to Christ's love, letting it bear fruit in them, so that they can, in turn, share this same *free, total, faithful, fruitful* love with each other.

Committing to love in this way has a name: it's called *marriage*. This, in fact, is precisely what a bride and groom commit to at the altar. The priest or deacon asks them: "Have you come here *freely* and *wholeheartedly* to give yourselves to each other in marriage? Do you promise to be *faithful* all the days of your lives? Do you promise to *receive children* lovingly from God?" When the bride and groom each say "yes," that word expresses the language of their hearts: this is what we want; this is what we desire—to love as Christ loves. In turn, spouses are meant to express that same "yes" of their hearts with the language of their bodies whenever they become one flesh. "In fact, the words themselves, 'I take you as my wife/as my husband,'" John Paul II says, "can only be fulfilled by . . . conjugal intercourse" (TOB 103:2).

In other words, sexual intercourse is where the words of the wedding vows *become flesh*. It's where husband and wife are meant to *incarnate* divine love. The Church's sexual ethic begins to make beautiful and compelling sense when understood in this divine light. The Church's teaching is not a prudish list of prohibitions. It's a call to embrace our own greatness, our own God-given dignity. It's a call to fulfill the Gospel call to love as Christ loves: "Husbands, love your wives, as Christ loved the church" (Eph 5:25).

No married couple, of course, will love each other perfectly in this regard. Pope Francis is right to acknowledge that the "language of the body calls for a patient apprenticeship in learning to interpret and channel desires in view of authentic self-giving." Hence, "there is no need to lay upon two limited persons the tremendous burden of having to reproduce perfectly the union between Christ and his Church, for marriage as a sign," Francis concludes, "advances gradually with the progressive integration of the gifts of God."[30] However, "what is known as 'the law of gradualness' or step-by-step advance," said John Paul II, "cannot be identified with 'gradualness of the law,' as if there were different degrees … in God's law for different individuals and situations."[31] To alter the divine law of love because it is difficult and we are imperfect is to maintain that it is acceptable in certain circumstances for couples to violate their wedding vows. This, in fact, is precisely what is at stake in upholding the teaching of *Humanae Vitae*.

Fidelity to the Wedding Vows

Spouses are free to choose whether to engage in sexual intercourse. But if they choose to do so, they are not free to change the meaning of their union. Fertility is not an afterthought in God's design for marital love. Rather, it "is present from the beginning of love as an essential feature, one that cannot be denied without disfiguring that love itself," observes Francis. "Hence," as he concludes, "no genital act of husband and wife can refuse this meaning."[32]

The language of sexual intercourse has "clearcut meanings," all of which are "programmed," John Paul II says, in the conjugal consent, in the vows. For example, to "the question: 'Are you ready to accept children lovingly from God? . . .' the man and the woman answer, 'Yes'" (TOB 105:6, 106:3). If spouses say "yes" at the altar, but then render their union sterile, they are lying with their bodies. They are being unfaithful to their wedding vows. Such dishonesty at the heart of the marital covenant cannot fail to have a deleterious effect both on individual couples and on a whole society's understanding of marriage.

Someone might retort, "Come on! I can commit to being 'open to children' at the altar, but this doesn't mean that *each* and *every* act of intercourse needs to be open to children." But that makes as much sense as saying, "Come on! I can commit to fidelity at the altar, but this doesn't mean that *each* and *every* act of intercourse needs to be with my spouse." If you can recognize the inconsistency of a commitment to fidelity, *but not always* . . . you can recognize the inconsistency of a commitment to being open to children, *but not always*.

Perhaps another way out of this logic is simply for a couple to exclude openness to children in the commitment they make at the altar. Then a couple wouldn't be lying with their bodies by using contraception, would they? It would reflect what they committed to (or didn't commit to), yes. But what they committed to would not be to love as God loves. What they committed to would not be marriage. And this is why the Church has always recognized that willfully excluding openness to children renders a marriage null from the start.

Responsible Parenthood

So, does fidelity to the wedding vows imply that couples are to leave the number of children they have entirely to chance? No. In calling couples to a responsible love, the Church calls them also to a responsible parenthood.

Pope Paul VI stated clearly that couples are considered "to exercise responsible parenthood who prudently and generously decide to have a large family, or who, for serious reasons and with due respect to the moral law, choose to have no more children for the time being or even for an indeterminate period."[33] Notice that large families should result from prudent reflection and generosity, not chance. Notice, too, that couples must have "serious reasons" to avoid pregnancy and must respect the moral law, the ethics of the sign.

Assuming a couple has a serious reason to avoid a child (this could be financial, physical, or psychological, among other reasons), what could they do that would not violate the consummate expression of their sacrament? In other words, what could they do to avoid conceiving a child that would not render them unfaithful to their wedding vows? I'll bet you're doing it right now. They could *abstain* from sex. If we understand the dignity of the human being and the astounding meaning of becoming one flesh, we will logically conclude, as the Church always has, that the only method of "birth control" in keeping with human dignity is self-control.

A further question arises: Would a couple be doing anything to falsify their sexual union if they embraced during a time of natural infertility? Take, for example, a couple past childbearing years. They know their union will not result in a child. Are they violating the sacramental sign of their marriage if they engage in intercourse with this knowledge? Are they contracepting? No. Contraception, by definition, is the choice to engage in an act of intercourse, but then do something else to *render* it sterile. This can be done by using various devices, hormones, surgical procedures, and the age-old method of withdrawal (*coitus interruptus*).

Couples who use natural family planning (NFP) when they have a just reason to avoid pregnancy *never* render their sexual acts sterile; they never contracept. They track their fertility, abstain when they are fertile, and if they so desire, embrace when they are naturally infertile. Readers unfamiliar with modern NFP methods should note that they are 98–99 percent effective at avoiding pregnancy when used properly. Furthermore, any woman, regardless of the regularity of her cycles, can use NFP successfully. This is not the outdated and much less precise "rhythm method."

What's the Difference?

To some people this seems like splitting hairs. "What's the big difference," they ask, "between rendering the union sterile yourself and just *waiting* until it's naturally infertile? The end result is the same thing: both couples avoid children." To which I respond, "What's the big difference between killing Grandma and just *waiting* until she dies naturally? The end result is the same thing: dead Grandma." Yes, the end result is the same, but one case involves a serious sin called murder, while in the other case, Grandma dies, but there's no sin involved. Give it some thought: if you can understand the difference between euthanasia and natural death, you can understand the difference between contraception and natural family planning.

John Paul II rightly observes that the difference between periodic abstinence (NFP) and contraception "is much wider and deeper than is usually thought, one which involves in the final analysis two irreconcilable concepts of the human person and of human sexuality."[34] The difference, in fact, is one of cosmic proportions.

First, it's important to recognize that the Church has never said it is inherently wrong to avoid children. But the end (avoiding children) does not justify the means. There may well be a good reason for you to wish Grandma would pass on to the next life. Perhaps she is suffering terribly with age and disease. But this does not justify killing her. Similarly, you may have a good reason to avoid conceiving a child. Perhaps you are in serious financial straits. Perhaps you have four kids under the age of four and you have reached your emotional limits. But no scenario justifies rendering the sexual act sterile, just as no scenario justifies killing Grandma.

Grandma's natural death and a woman's natural period of infertility are both acts of God. But in killing Grandma or in rendering sex sterile, we take the powers of life *into our own hands*—just like the deceiver originally tempted us to do—and we make ourselves like God (see Gen 3:5). Therefore, as John Paul II concludes, "Contraception is to be judged so profoundly unlawful as never to be, for any reason, justified. To think or to say the contrary is equal to maintaining that in human life, situations may arise in which it is lawful not to recognize God as God."[35]

Love or Lust?

One of the main objections to *Humanae Vitae* is that following its teaching (that is, practicing periodic abstinence when avoiding pregnancy) impedes couples from expressing their love for one another. Let's take a closer look at this objection.

First of all, it is true that abstaining from sex for the wrong reasons (out of spite for a spouse, or out of disdain for sex, for example) is damaging to marital love. But as every married couples knows, abstaining from sex for the right reasons can be a profound act of love. Indeed, there are many occasions in married life when a couple might *want* to renew their wedding vows through intercourse, but love demands they abstain: maybe one of the spouses is sick; maybe it's after childbirth; maybe they're at the in-laws and there are thin walls; or maybe the couple has a serious reason to avoid a child. In these cases, and in many others, if a couple can't abstain, their love is called into question.

God is the one who united marital love and procreation. Therefore, since God cannot contradict himself, a "true contradiction cannot exist between the divine laws pertaining to the transmission of life and those pertaining to authentic conjugal love."[36] It may well be difficult to follow the teaching of *Humanae Vitae*, but it could never be a contradiction of love. Following this teaching is difficult because authentic love is difficult. In each of us, there is an internal battle between love and lust (true eros and the distortions thereof). Lust impels us, and impels us very powerfully, toward sexual activity.

However, if this activity results from nothing more than a desire we can't direct or control, it's not love we're expressing; it's love's opposite: use. In reality, what we often call love "if subjected to searching critical examination turns out to be, contrary to all appearances, only a form of 'utilization' of the person."[37]

What purpose does contraception really serve? This might sound odd at first, but let it sink in. Contraception was not invented to prevent pregnancy. We already had a 100 percent safe, 100 percent reliable way of doing that—*abstinence*. In the final analysis, contraception serves only one purpose: to spare us the difficulty we experience when confronted with the choice of abstinence. When all the smoke is cleared, contraception was invented because of our lack of self-control; in other words, contraception was invented to serve the indulgence of lust. Why do we spay or neuter our dogs and cats? Why don't we just ask them to abstain? If we spay and neuter ourselves through contraceptive practices, we are reducing the "great mystery" of the one-flesh union to the level of animals in heat. And this is why contracepted intercourse not only attacks the procreative meaning of sex, "it also *ceases to be an act of love*" (TOB 123:6).

Paraphrasing insights from Dr. Greg Popcak, we need to recognize that any frustration we feel in practicing the abstinence required of NFP is a sign that NFP is doing the job it's meant to do: it's helping us grow in virtue and authentic freedom. When we feel those frustrations, we must learn to recognize them as the growing pains of personal maturity and the capacity for expressing authentic love. In those times when the growing pains hurt the most, we're not feeling a sexual urge that must be satisfied, but a selfish urge that must be transformed if we are to reclaim the freedom that our fallenness has taken from us. This is the gift and role of true chastity.

Chastity and the Integration of Love

Chastity, so often considered "negative" or "repressive," is supremely positive and liberating. It's the virtue that frees sexual desire from the utilitarian attitude, from the tendency to use others for our own gratification. Chastity requires "an *apprenticeship in self-mastery* which is a training in human freedom. The alternative is clear: either man governs his passions and finds peace, or he lets himself be dominated by them and becomes unhappy" (CCC 2339).

There is an undeniable "tension," "struggle," and "difficulty" for human beings in the basic fact that genitals are made for generating. To relieve that struggle, we either need to learn how to control our genitals or how to control their ability to generate: one or the other. With modern means of contraception and abortion at our ready disposal, there is no question which route is easier. But are those who cannot control their sexual desires free, or are they enslaved? Is freedom *license to indulge our compulsions*, or is freedom *liberation from our compulsions to indulge*?

Self-mastery does not merely mean resisting our compulsions by force of will. That's only the negative side of the picture. As we mature in self-mastery, we experience it as "*the ability to orient* [sexual] reactions both as to their content and as to their character" (TOB 129:5). The person who is truly chaste is able to direct erotic desire "toward what is true, good, and beautiful, so that what is 'erotic' also becomes true, good, and beautiful" (TOB 48:1). As spouses experience liberation from compulsion, they enter into the true freedom of self-giving, which enables them to express the language of their bodies "in a depth, simplicity, and beauty hitherto altogether unknown" (TOB 117b:5).

It's certainly true that chastity requires "asceticism," understood as a ready and determined willingness to resist the impulses of lust. But authentic chastity does not repress sexual desire. It submits it to Christ's death and Resurrection. The more lust dies, the more authentic love is raised up. As John Paul II expresses it, "If conjugal chastity (and chastity in general) manifests itself at first as an ability to resist [lust], it subsequently reveals itself as a *singular ability* to perceive, love, and realize those meanings of the 'language of the body' that remain completely unknown to [lust] itself" (TOB 128:3). Hence, the discipline required by chastity does not impoverish or impede a couple's expressions of love and affection. Rather, "it makes them spiritually more intense and thus *enriches* them" (TOB 128:3).

Marital Spirituality

Such chastity, John Paul II says, stands at the center of the spirituality of marriage (see TOB 131:2). What is marital spirituality? It involves spouses opening themselves to the indwelling power of the Holy Spirit and allowing him to guide them in all their choices and behaviors. John Paul II says that sexual union itself—with all its emotional joys and physical pleasures—is meant to be an expression of "life according to the Spirit" (see TOB 101:6). When spouses are open to the gift, the Holy Spirit infuses their sexual desires "with everything that is noble and beautiful," with "the supreme value which is love" (TOB 46:5). But when spouses close themselves off to the Holy Spirit, sexual union quickly degenerates into an act of mutual exploitation.

Without the Holy Spirit, human weakness makes the teaching of *Humanae Vitae* a burden no one can bear. But to whom is this teaching given? To men and women enslaved by their weaknesses? Or to men and women set free by the *power* of the Holy Spirit? This is what is at stake in the teaching of *Humanae Vitae*—the power of the Gospel! The Church holds out the teaching of *Humanae Vitae* with absolute confidence in the fact that "God's love has been poured into our hearts by the Holy Spirit who has been given to us" (Rom 5:5).

Married couples "must implore [God] for such 'power' and for every other 'divine help' in prayer . . . they must draw grace and love from the ever-living fountain of the Eucharist; . . . 'with humble perseverance' they must overcome their own faults and sins in the sacrament of Penance. These are the means—*infallible and indispensable*—to form the Christian spirituality of conjugal . . . life" (TOB 126:5). All of which, of course, presupposes faith understood as the openness of the human heart to the gift of the Holy Spirit.

If spouses are not living an authentic spirituality—in other words, if their hearts aren't open to the transforming power of the Holy Spirit—they will tend to view the Church's teaching against contraception as an oppressive rule imposed by an oppressive Church. On the other hand, spouses who engage in their sexual embrace as an expression of life according to the Holy Spirit recognize the Church's teaching as the path to the love and freedom for which they yearn. In turn, they are filled with a profound reverence for what comes from God, which shapes their spirituality "*for the sake of protecting the particular dignity of [the sexual] act*" (TOB 132:2).

Such spouses understand that their union is meant to signify and participate in God's creative and redeeming love. In other words, they understand the theology of their bodies. And being filled with a deep "veneration for *the essential values of conjugal union*" saves them from "violating or degrading what bears in itself the sign of the divine mystery of creation and redemption" (TOB 131:5). John Paul II observes that life in the Holy Spirit leads couples to understand, among all the possible manifestations of love and affection, "the singular, and even exceptional meaning" of the sexual embrace (TOB 132:2). However, contraceptive practice—and the mentality behind it—demonstrates a serious lack of understanding of the meaning of the sexual embrace in God's plan. Such a lack, John Paul II maintained, constitutes in a way the antithesis of marital spirituality (see TOB 132:2).

How so? If marital spirituality involves spouses opening their bodies—and the one body they become in the sexual act—to the Holy Spirit, contraception marks a specific closing off of their bodies to the Holy Spirit. Who is the Holy Spirit? As we say in the Nicene Creed, he is "the Lord, the Giver of Life." What does contracepted sex say, if not: "Lord and Giver of Life, we do not want you to be part of this act"?

Most couples who use contraception simply have no idea what they are doing or saying with their bodies.

They haven't ever heard or understood the "great mystery" of their sexuality. Hence, the conclusions we're drawing here about the objective seriousness of contraception is not a matter of assigning culpability: "Father, forgive them; for they know not what they do" (Luke 23:34). The good news is that Christ came into the world not to condemn but to save (see John 3:17). It doesn't matter how much lust has dominated a person's life. It doesn't matter how "dyslexic" or even "illiterate" a person has been in reading the divine language of the body. As John Paul II boldly proclaims, through the gift of God's mercy "there is always the possibility of passing from 'error' to the 'truth' . . . the possibility of . . . conversion from sin to chastity as an expression of a life according to the Spirit" (TOB 107:3).

THE THIRD SECRET
OF FATIMA

The "third secret" of Fatima was shrouded in mystery for eighty-three years. In the year 2000, at the beatification ceremony of two of the young visionaries to whom Mary appeared (Francesco and Jacinta), Pope St. John Paul II finally unveiled it. In 1917, the three children had seen a vision of bullets and arrows fired at "a bishop dressed in white."

Sixty-four years later, while driving through the crowd in St. Peter's Square, a "bishop dressed in white" was indeed gunned down by Turkish assassin Ali Agca . . . *on the memorial of Our Lady of Fatima*: May 13, 1981. Thankfully, while the bishop in the vision fell dead, John Paul II miraculously survived. Many years later the pope himself reflected: "Agca knew how to shoot, and he certainly shot to kill. Yet it was as if someone was guiding and deflecting that bullet." That "someone," John Paul believed, was the Woman of Fatima. "Could I forget that the event in Saint Peter's

Square took place on the day and at the hour when the first appearance of the Mother of Christ . . . has been remembered . . . at Fatima in Portugal? For in everything that happened to me on that very day, I felt that extraordinary motherly protection and care, which turned out to be stronger than the deadly bullet."[38]

The fact that John Paul II was shot on the memorial of Fatima is well known. What few people realize is that the pope was planning to announce the establishment of his Institute for Studies on Marriage and Family on that fateful afternoon. This was to be his main arm for disseminating his Theology of the Body around the globe. Could it be that there were forces at work that didn't want John Paul II's teaching to spread around the world? (In fact, by May 13, 1981, John Paul II was only about halfway through delivering the 129 addresses of his TOB. Had he died, obviously the full teaching never would have been presented.) And could it be that, by saving his life, the Woman of Fatima was pointing to the importance of his teaching reaching the world?

It would be over a year later that John Paul II officially established his Institute (of which I'm a proud graduate). On that day, October 7, 1982—not coincidentally the Feast of Our Lady of the Rosary—John Paul II entrusted the Pontifical Institute for Studies on Marriage and Family to the care and protection of Our Lady of Fatima. By doing so, he himself was drawing a connection between his miraculous survival and the importance of the Theology of the Body. "Precisely because the family is threatened, the family is being attacked, so the Pope must be attacked," he would write some years later. "The Pope must suffer, so that the world may see that there is a higher gospel, as it were, the gospel of suffering, by which the future is prepared, the third millennium of families."[39]

If the third millennium is to be the "millennium of families," it's an understatement to say we're not off to a very good start. It was then-Father (now Cardinal) Carlo Caffarra, in his role as president of the above-mentioned Pontifical Institute, to whom Sister Lucia had written in the early 1980s: "Father, a time will come when the decisive battle between the kingdom of Christ and Satan will be over marriage and the family." She added, however, that there was no need to be afraid "because Our Lady has already crushed his head."[40] In May 2017, just a few months before his own death, Caffarra stated: "What Sister Lucia wrote to me is being fulfilled today."[41]

The Triumph of Purity of Heart

At the start of this essay, we learned that the errors of Russia go deeper than communism: at the heart of the Marxist worldview is a calculated attempt to eliminate the purpose of gender—that of generating children—so that the male-female distinction itself becomes culturally irrelevant, thus destroying the anthropological basis of marriage and the family. There is no doubt that this error has taken hold of much of the world and continues to spread today at rampant speed. But here's the good news: just as John Paul II's vision of the human person inaugurated a revolution that led to the fall of communism, that same vision has the potential to topple today's sexual ideology (or, shall we say, asexual ideology) as well. It is called the Theology of the Body and it has already started a movement that is spreading from heart to heart around the world.

In a 2005 interview, Lech Walesa, who led the movement in Poland against communism, reflected on the revolution of conscience that John Paul II ignited: "For twenty years I could only find ten people who wanted to fight [the communist regime], from a nation of forty million. Nobody, I repeat, nobody thought that communism would end. Then, this incredible thing happened—a Pole became . . . the pope. And within a year after his visit to Poland [in June 1979]—in one year—it went from ten people to a movement of ten million."[42]

The political philosopher Zbigniew Stawrowski reflected on the experience of the Polish people after John Paul II's historic visit to his homeland:

When we are talking about a revolution of conscience, we are talking about people who suddenly asked themselves: "Who am I? What am I doing here? What is the purpose of my life?" We lived within something that was permeated by the feeling of nonsense. We fully realized that it was false, that it was a lie, one huge lie. However, you were trapped in it. And suddenly someone arrives who says, "No! There's no need to lie any longer."[43]

In the same way, today's gender ideology (more aptly, genderless ideology) is based on a lie. And lies eventually collapse on themselves, doomed from the start by their own falsity. We are now in the umbra of the eclipse of the body, but the light of truth will emerge, perhaps sooner than we think. In the book of Revelation the sexual distortion of the nations—symbolized by the "whore of Babylon," that mysterious feminine figure who mocks the Bride of the Lamb and seduces the world with her harlotry—is brought to ruin in "one hour" (see Rev 18:10-17). And then comes the triumph of the New Jerusalem, the Bride who has "made herself ready" for her Bridegroom. She is dressed in fine linen, bright and *immaculate* (see Rev 19:7–8). She is "clothed with the sun" (Rev 12:1).

This radiant Bride, in other words, magnifies the light of the sun rather than eclipses it. And let us not overlook this illuminating detail: the Bride in the book of Revelation is *pregnant* . . . (see Rev 12:2). John Paul II pointed out the difference between the Bride and "the hostile and furious presence" of Babylon as follows: the woman clothed with the sun "is endowed with an inner fruitfulness by which she constantly brings forth children of God." In contrast, Babylon embodies "death and inner barrenness."[44] In fact, this feminine figure *prefers* barrenness. She *chooses* it and seduces the nations with the promise of sexual pleasure without sacrifice (which is to say, without divine love).

The pregnant Bride in the Book of Revelation, of course, is personified in Mary, the same woman who promised the children of Fatima: "In the end, my Immaculate Heart will triumph." What does this mean? In short, it means that *purity of heart* will triumph. As Cardinal Ratzinger explained in his official commentary on the third secret: "According to Matthew 5:8 ['Blessed are the pure of heart, for they shall see God'], the 'immaculate heart' is a heart which, with God's grace, has come to perfect interior unity and therefore 'sees God.' To be 'devoted' to the Immaculate Heart of Mary means therefore to embrace this attitude of heart, which makes the fiat—'your will be done'—the defining center of one's whole life."[45]

Purity is not prudishness or fear of the body and its genital functions. Purity, says John Paul II, "is the glory of the human body before God. It is the glory of God in the human body, through which masculinity and femininity are manifested" (TOB 57:3). Those who are pure of heart are those who have followed Christ's invitation to "Come, and become one who sees" (John 1:39). And what they *see* is the fact that human sexuality "bears in itself the sign of the divine mystery of creation and redemption" (TOB 131:5). What they see is the fact that the body, in fact, and only the body, is capable of making visible what is invisible: the spiritual and divine. It has been created to transfer into the visible reality of the world the mystery hidden from eternity in God, and thus to be a sign of it (TOB 19:4).

The Era of Peace Will Come Through the Cross

At the top of page 1 of the original handwritten manuscript of John Paul II's TOB is the dedication: *tota pulchra es Maria* (Mary, you are all beautiful), and below that is the date he started writing it: December 8, 1974. Is it merely a coincidence that John Paul II began writing his TOB on the feast of the Immaculate Conception? Right from the start, it seems, John Paul II's TOB is mysteriously connected with the triumph of Mary's Immaculate Heart.

Of course, we do not know when these prophecies will be fulfilled, be they biblical prophecies or the Church-approved prophesies of Fatima. But John Paul II himself had already written in 1994 that the latter "seem to be close to their fulfillment."[46] This much is certain: since the family is the fundamental cell of society, if an "era of peace" is to be granted the world, that peace can only come if there is peace in the marital relationship . . . in the womb . . . in the family. And this will only happen if we are reconciled to the truth of our own greatness as men and women who bear in our bodies the sacramental sign of the divine plan—a plan that inevitably leads us to the nuptial mystery of the Cross.

As the icon of divine love, marriage has been under attack since the beginning. In fact, as John Paul II observed, "Sin and death have entered into man's history *in some way through the very heart of that unity that had from the 'beginning' been formed by man and woman,* created and called to become 'one flesh' (Gen 2:24)" (TOB 20:1). But if the enemy entered the sanctuary of married life from the beginning to sow seeds of death and destruction, let us never forget where Christ performed his first miracle: "On *the third day,* there was a wedding in Cana" (John 2:1 NABRE). And let us also remember that that wedding was a foreshadowing of the "hour" of Christ's death. Unfathomable as it is to human wisdom, this is God's method of victory: the death and Resurrection of the Bridegroom is the gift that assures the triumph of the Bride.

We must ponder this anew if we are to understand what is happening in our world today: marriage, it would seem, is going the way of its exemplar. It's already been put on trial, condemned, mocked, rejected, spat upon, scourged, and it's now being crucified. Significantly, on the day of Christ's Crucifixion, Luke reports that "darkness came over the whole land . . . because of an eclipse of the sun" (Luke 23:45 NABRE). Thereafter, Christ's body—the light that illuminates the meaning of our bodies—was placed in the darkness of the tomb.

Many in the Church today are understandably fearful and anxious because of the darkness that is descending upon us. Three astronomers—Our Lady of Fatima, Pope Paul VI, and St. John Paul II—have enabled us to understand what's happening. As with every eclipse, the eclipse of the body is sure to get darker before it gets lighter. The truth proclaimed by Paul VI in *Humanae Vitae* and explained so compellingly by John Paul II in his Theology of the Body remains a sign of contradiction fiercely resisted not only by the world at large, but also by strong forces within the Church. A new wave of attacks against this truth may well bring fresh defeats for the Body of Christ and for humanity.

None of this should be surprising. For the Church must "follow her Lord in his death and Resurrection" in order to enter her glory, as the *Catechism* observes (CCC 677). We know not the day nor the hour of Christ's return, but this we do know: "Before Christ's second coming the Church must pass through a final trial that will shake the faith of many believers. The persecution that accompanies her pilgrimage on earth will unveil the 'mystery of iniquity' in the form of a religious deception offering men an apparent solution to their problems at the price of apostasy from the truth" (CCC 675).

While we can't conclude with any certainty that we are now facing this final trial, it is eerily curious how precisely contraception fits the bill of this "religious deception." With all the forces of darkness arrayed against her teaching, we should not expect "a historic triumph of the Church." Rather, by accepting "the way" of death and resurrection, we will witness "God's victory over the final unleashing of evil, which will cause his Bride to come down from heaven" (CCC 677).

As the eclipse of the body continues to cast its dark shadow over the world, let us take courage: *Sun*-day is not far off. When "the third day" dawns, the body will be rebirthed from the darkness of the tomb (or, shall we say, womb) and there will be a miraculous wedding: the sun will come forth "like a bridegroom from his canopy" and nothing will escape its heat (see Ps 19:6–7); and another great sign will appear in the sky, the Immaculate Woman, clothed with the sun, showing the world what it means to *open bodily* to the divine fire of life-giving love. "Then the glory of the Lord shall be revealed, and all flesh shall see it together" (Isa 40:5 NABRE).

Let it be, Lord, according to your word. Amen.

Suggestions for further study

- If you have the aptitude, read John Paul II's actual text: *Man and Woman He Created Them: A Theology of the Body* (Boston: Pauline, 2006). If you need help with that, read it in conjunction with my extended commentary, *Theology of the Body Explained*, or my *Theology of the Body for Beginners*. Visit my ministry's website corproject.com and click on "shop" for a full listing of additional resources.

- Explore what other authors and teachers have written about the TOB. There are so many good resources out there today, each with their own emphases and insights. Google "theology of the body resources" to find them.

- If you would like ongoing formation in the TOB, consider joining a worldwide community of men and women who are learning, living, and sharing the TOB as Members of the Cor Project. Visit cormembership.com to learn more.

- Consider taking a five-day Immersion Course through the Theology of the Body Institute. Learn more at tobinstitute.org.

- For more in-depth study, consider the Theology of the Body Institute's Certification Program or the graduate degree programs offered by the Pontifical John Paul II Institute for Studies on Marriage and Family.

Support the Global Mission of Theology of the Body Institute

You Are Invited to Join Us

The TOBI Patron Community gathers enthusiasts from around the world who want to live, learn and share St. John Paul II's Theology of the Body teachings. In addition to supporting the global works of the Institute, patrons have access to exclusive formation and other great perks!

As A Patron

- *You Make Our Work Possible.*
- *You Are Part of a Community*
- *You Are a Defender of Truth.*
  - *You Are a Gift to Us.*

Our Gift to You

- *Vast Library of Videos & Audio Talks*
  - *Online Study Programs*
  - *Exclusive Virtual Retreats*
    - *Virtual Pilgrimages*
  - *Past Virtual Conferences*
- *OTHER GREAT PERKS AS A PATRON!*

Become A Patron At
WWW.TOBPATRON.COM

Or take a **photo of the dinosaur** *to learn more*

Obtain copies of this book
and others like it, for **$3 in bulk!**

To order, visit:

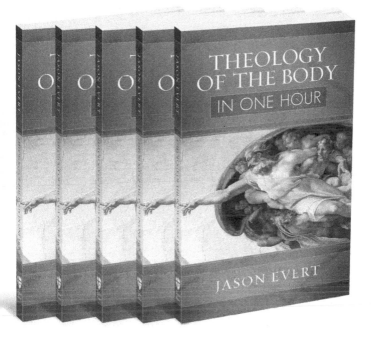

Obtain copies of this book
and others like it, for **$3 in bulk!**

To order, visit:

Teach the Theology of the Body to Teens!

YOU: Life, Love, and the Theology of the Body (High school program)

Theology of the Body for Teens: Middle School edition

Theology of His Body / Theology of Her Body

To order these resources or donate to our ministry, please visit:

Learn more about the Theology of the Body!

- **The Cor Project** is a global membership and outreach organization founded by Christopher West devoted to helping men and women learn, live, and share the Theology of the Body in compelling, life-transforming ways. Visit Corproject.com.

- **Dumb Ox Ministries** works with teens, young adults, and families; cultivating their authentic masculinity and femininity through the Theology of the Body, helping them to prepare for, discern, and pursue their unique vocations to love. Visit dumboxministries.com.

- **Into the Deep** provides outdoor Theology of the Body Retreats with Jen Messing. Visit idretreats.org.

- **JOYTOB** is the international teaching ministry of Damon Owens, offering Theology of the Body seminars, conferences, retreats, and parish missions. Visit joytob.org.

- **Pontifical John Paul II Institute for Studies on Marriage and Family** was established by Saint John Paul II as a theological center devoted to the study of the Church's teaching on marriage and the family. It offers accredited pontifical degree programs, as well as civilly accredited graduate degree programs (master's, license, and doctoral-level education). Visit johnpaulii.edu.

- **Ruah Woods** exists to restore the family and renew the culture by educating and training leaders and teachers to understand, embrace, and evangelize the message of Theology of the Body. Visit ruahwoods.org.

- **Tabor Life Institute** is dedicated to promoting the sacramental-liturgical worldview of the human person and the entire created order. Their mission is to help transform lives through the Theology of the Body. Visit taborlife.org.

- **Theology of the Body Evangelization Team (TOBET)** promotes the Theology of the Body through programs and resources designed for people of all ages. Visit tobet.org.

- **TheologyOfTheBody.net** offers audio and video presentations, books, articles, and other resources to learn about the Theology of the Body from a wide range of speakers and authors.

- **The Theology of the Body Institute** spreads the message of Theology of the Body through retreats, talks, graduate level courses, and clergy enrichment training for men and women of every vocation and walk of life. Visit TOBinstitute.org.

1   My thanks to Daniel Moody for this turn of phrase. See *The Flesh Made Word: A New Reason to be Against Abortion* (n.p.: Amazon, 2016).

2   As cited in in Walter J. Schu, *The Splendor of Love: John Paul II's Vision for Marriage and Family* (New Hope, KY: New Hope Publications, 2003).

3   Sister Lucia wrote these words in a letter to the late Cardinal Carlo Caffarra, when he served as president of the John Paul II Institute for Studies on Marriage and Family. Caffarra has given sworn testimony that these were, in fact, her words. See https://aleteia.org/2017/05/19/exclusive-cardinal-caffarra-what-sr-lucia-wrote-to-me-is-being-fulfilled-today/.

4   Pope Pius XI, *On Chaste Marriage*, paragraph 56.

5   Second Vatican Council, *Gaudium et Spes*, section 51, endnote 14.

6   See Pope Paul VI homily at Fatima, Portugal, May 13, 1967.

7   See Pope Paul VI, *Humanae Vitae* 17.

8   Sigmund Freud, *Introductory Lectures in Psychoanalysis* (New York: W. W. Norton and Company, 1966), p. 392.

9   See James D. Richardson, *A Compilation of the Messages and Papers of the Presidents*, Volume XI (Washington, D.C.: Bureau of National Literature and Art, 1908).

10 Mahatma Gandhi, *India of My Dreams* (New Delhi: Rajpal & Sons, 2009), pp. 219–220.

11 *Washington Post*, "Forgetting Religion," March 22, 1931.

12 See T.S. Eliot, *Thoughts After Lambeth* (London: Faber & Faber, 1931).

13 Rowan D. Williams, "The Body's Grace," in *Theology and Sexuality: Classic and Contemporary Readings*, ed. Eugene F. Rogers, Jr. (London: Blackwell, 2002), p. 320.

14 Joseph Cardinal Ratzinger with Vittorio Messori, *The Ratzinger Report* (San Francisco: Ignatius Press, 1985), pp. 85, 95.

15 John Paul II actually divided his manuscript into 135 talks. However, some of the content of his reflections on the Song of Songs was considered too "delicate" for the Wednesday audience format, so he condensed 10 talks in that section to four, thus delivering only 129. For an extended treatment of the undelivered talks, see my book *Heaven's Song* (West Chester: Ascension Press, 2008).

16 *Humanae Vitae* 7.

17 John 1:39 is typically rendered as "Come and see." As I once learned in my biblical studies (from those much more learned than I on such matters), the more accurate rendering of Christ's words is "Come, and become one who sees."

18 Pope John Paul II, *Mulieris Dignitatem* 26.

19 Pope Benedict XVI, *Deus Caritas Est* 9.

20 Pope Benedict XVI, Lenten Message 2007.

21 Pope Benedict XVI, *Deus Caritas Est* 10.

22 St. Bonaventure, *Bringing Forth Christ: Five Feasts of the Child Jesus* (Oxford: Fairacres Publication, 1884).

23 St. Augustine, Sermon 291.

24 See Pope John Paul II, *Letter to Familias* 10.

25 See, for example, Pope John Paul II, *Novo Millennio Inuente* 33.

26 Henry Dieterich, *Through the Year with Bishop Fulton Sheen* (San Francisco: Ignatius Press, 2003), p. 60.

27 Pope Benedict XVI, Lenten Message 2007.

28 Pope John Paul II, *Mulieris Dignitatem* 26.

29 Pope John Paul II, *Letter to Families* 23.

30 Pope Francis, *Amoris Laetitia* 284, 122.

31 Pope John Paul II, *Familiaris Consortio* 34.

32 Pope Francis, *Amoris Laetitia* 80.

33 Pope Paul VI, *Humanae Vitae* 10.

34 Pope John Paul II, *Familiaris Consortio* 32.

35 Pope John Paul II, Address, October 10, 1983.

36 Second Vatican Council, *Gaudium et Spes* 51.

37 Karol Wojtyla, *Love and Responsibility* (San Francisco: Ignatius Press, 1993), p. 167.

38 Pope John Paul II, *Memory and Identity* (Waterville, ME: Thorndike Press, 2006), pp. 159, 163.

39 Pope John Paul II, Angelus Message, May 29, 1994 (my thanks to Jason Evert for pointing this out to me).

40 See note 3.

41 Ibid.

42 "John Paul II: Ambassador of Peace" (Discovery Channel, 2005).

43 *Liberating a Continent: John Paul II and the Fall of Communism*, documentary directed by David Naglieri (Goya Producciones and PBS, 2016).

44 Pope John Paul II, "The Church: A Bride Adorned for Her Husband," General Audience address, February 7, 2001.

45 Congregation for the Doctrine of the Faith "The Message of Fatima," http://www.vatican.va/roman_curia/congregations/cfaith/documents/rc_con_cfaith_doc_20000626_message-fatima_en.html.

46 Pope John Paul II, *Crossing the Threshold of Hope* (New York: Alfred A. Knopf, 1994), p. 221.

CPSIA information can be obtained
at www.ICGtesting.com
Printed in the USA
LVHW012308190821
695619LV00004B/7